Did you know . . .
that you cannot see yourself sneeze?

Y0-DBS-886

Know why? Because you always close your eyes when you sneeze! Everyone sneezes, from the richest right down to the poorest. When something gets into your nose which does not belong there, like dust or pepper, you sneeze. There are several thousand tiny **particles** carried inside the water. They blast out of your nose and mouth when you sneeze. These particles can carry germs, disease, and dirt. So, when you sneeze, cover up your nose and mouth. It is not just to be **polite**, it is for your own good health!

1. **Underline the best title for this paragraph:**
   Ahhhhhh-Chooo
   Keep Your Eyes Shut
   Try Keeping Your Eyes Open

2. **Circle the answers you think are correct:**
   You cover your mouth when you sneeze only because it is
   the polite thing to do.   Yes   No
   Sneezing is always caused by a cold.   Yes   No

3. **Circle the correct meaning for each underlined word:**
   particles
   (par′ ti cles)

   a. tiny pieces of something
   b. germs
   c. dirt

   polite
   (po lité)

   a. quiet
   b. nice, correct
   c. party

achoo!

?

Did you know . . .
that the oldest winter sport in the Olympics is figure skating?

Long before men could read or write, they went ice skating. But at that time ice skating was not a sport for fun. It was an important means of **transportation** in the winter. The first ice skates were made from the bones of animals. It was not until about 500 years ago that metals were used to make ice skates. A lot of the **development** of ice skating and ice skates took place in the country of Holland. The Dutch used ice skates to get from one village to another on the frozen **canals.**

1. **Underline the best title for this paragraph:**
   Ice Skating Just for Fun
   Ice Skating Wasn't Just for Fun
   Figure Skating

2. **Circle the answers you think are correct:**
   The first men who ice skated could read and write.   Yes   No
   The first ice skates were made of metal.   Yes   No

3. **Circle the correct meaning for each underlined word:**
   transportation
   (trans por ta′ tion)
      a. getting from one place to another
      b. getting across frozen ice
      c. getting around in the winter

   development
   (de vel′op ment)
      a. birth
      b. death
      c. growth

   canals
   (ca nals′)
      a. rivers
      b. man-made waterways
      c. man-made metals

Did you know . . . stilts have been used all over the world since ancient times?

Long ago, in a **soggy** part of France, everyone wore stilts. Shepherds watched over their sheep on stilts. Housewives did their shopping on stilts. The children went to school, did their **chores**, and even played their games on stilts. We think of wearing stilts today as a fun thing to do. However, many people wear stilts for the **serious** business of picking fruit, making buildings, and even washing windows.

1. **Underline the best title for this paragraph:**
   Soggy Frenchmen
   A Fun Thing to Wear
   Wearing Stilts

2. **Circle the answers you think are correct:**
   People wear stilts just for fun today.   Yes   No
   Stilts were invented only about 100 years ago.   Yes   No

3. **Circle the correct meaning for each underlined word:**
   soggy
   (sog′gy)

   a. very hilly
   b. very wet
   c. very high

   chores
   a. jobs which must be done most every day
   b. jobs which are not fun to do
   c. jobs which are fun to do

   serious
   (se′ri ous)

   a. sad
   b. silly
   c. important, not funny

I wonder how they carried their books.

Did you know . . .
that basketball was almost named boxball?

In 1891, a gym **instructor** **invented** a game for his boys to play between the football and baseball seasons. He asked the janitor at the school to nail up a box at each end of the gym. The janitor could not find two boxes, so he nailed up two baskets instead. That is why we have basketball instead of boxball. Not everyone liked basketball at first. Now only ten boys could use the gym at a time. Over the years people have learned to enjoy watching and playing basketball. Now girls as well as boys like to play this game.

1. **Underline the best title for this paragraph:**
   Two Balls
   Two Boxes
   The Beginning of Basketball

2. **Fill in the blanks with the correct answers:**
   Basketball began in the year of _____.
   A _____ hung up baskets instead of boxes.

3. **Circle the correct meaning for each underlined word:**
   instructor
   (in struc′tor)

       a. a gym teacher
       b. a basketball teacher
       c. a teacher

   invented
   (in vent′ed)
       a. made up for the first time
       b. built
       c. made up for fun

Did you know . . .
Americans eat more than 2 million dollars' worth of popcorn at the movies in one year?

Popcorn is grown **mainly** in the Midwest states of Iowa, Nebraska, and Indiana. It grows well in these states partly because of the hot summers. Old timers tell of one summer when it was so hot that the popcorn in the fields started popping on the **stalks.** The pigs and cows thought they were in a **blizzard** and laid down and froze to death! Do you believe that?

1. **Underline the best title for this paragraph:**
   Eating Popcorn
   Growing Popcorn
   Popping Popcorn

2. **Fill in the blanks with the correct answer:**
   Popcorn is grown in the _____.
   A lot of popcorn is eaten each year at the _____.

3. **Circle the correct meaning for each underlined word:**
   mainly
   (main′ly)

   a. sometimes
   b. mostly
   c. all the time

   stalks

   a. leaves of plants
   b. roots of plants
   c. long stems of plants

   blizzard
   (bliz′zard)

   a. a hail storm
   b. a snow storm
   c. a rain storm

Did you know . . .
that "Witches Ring" mushrooms always grow in a circle?

Sometimes these kinds of mushrooms are called "fairy rings." A long time ago people believed that fairies danced around these rings of mushrooms. There are also many other kinds of mushrooms. You may have seen them in the grass or under a tree after a wet night. Many **varieties** of mushrooms are **edible,** but some can be very poisonous. Mushrooms don't make their own food but live off dead wood or plants. They grow and are picked all over the United States and Europe. Then they are canned and sold as a **delicious** food.

1. **Underline the best title for this paragraph:**
   A Ring of Mushrooms
   All About Mushrooms
   Growing Mushrooms

2. **Fill in the blanks with the correct answers:**
   Mushrooms live off _____ material.
   Mushrooms sometimes grow in a _____.

3. **Circle the correct meaning for each underlined word:**
   varieties
   (va ri′eties)

   a. vegetables
   b. kinds
   c. colors

   edible
   (ed′i ble)

   a. able to be grown
   b. able to be sold
   c. able to be eaten

   delicious
   (de li′cious)

   a. very good tasting
   b. very good looking
   c. very easy to grow

Did you know . . .
that mistletoe is not picked? It is shot down!

That's right! Mistletoe grows high up in trees. It **attaches** itself to trees like maple, elm, or apple, which lose their leaves each **autumn**. The small roots of mistletoe grow into the tree rather than into the ground like most other plants. It takes water from the tree. It gets the other food it needs from its leaves. In the late fall, it is either shot down or taken down with long forks, so that you can enjoy kissing under it at Christmas time.

1. **Underline the best title for this paragraph:**
   Kissing Under the Mistletoe
   It Grows on Trees!
   Shooting It Down

2. **Fill in the blanks with the correct answers:**
   We hang mistletoe up in the month of _____.
   Name three trees mistletoe might like to grow on.
   _____
   _____
   _____

3. **Circle the correct meaning for each underlined word:**
   attaches
   (at taches´)

   a. attacks
   b. hooks itself to
   c. lives in

   autumn
   (au´tumn)
   a. the season between summer and winter
   b. the season between winter and spring
   c. the season between spring and summer

I'd rather shoot it down than kiss under it!

Did you know . . .
that peanuts are used to make **dynamite?**

Not only are peanuts good to eat, they are used to make dynamite for explosions. Peanuts are grown in the southern United States. About half are made into peanut butter. Long ago peanuts grew only in South America. They were not planted here to sell until about 200 years ago. During the Civil War Northern soldiers fighting in the South found they liked eating peanuts. So their **popularity** grew. Today thousands of peanuts are planted each year. They are used for peanut butter, for eating, and for making other things . . . like dynamite.

1. **Underline the best title for this paragraph:**
    Peanuts for This and That
    An Explosive Plant
    Just for Peanut Butter

2. **Fill in the blanks with the correct answers:**
    Peanuts are used to make _____ _____.
    _____ soldiers liked to eat peanuts during the Civil

    War.

3. **Circle the correct meaning for each underlined word:**
    dynamite
    (dy'na mite)

    > a. used to make explosions
    > b. WOW!!
    > c. used to make peanuts

    popularity
    (pop u lar'ity)

    > a. to be eaten for enjoyment
    > b. to be well liked by many
    > c. to be well liked by one or two

Did you know . . . that green plants grow on the fur of the three-toed sloth?

That is true! Small green plants grow on the fur of this very slow-moving animal. When he hangs from trees, he looks more like **moss** than an animal. That keeps him safe from other larger animals. The sloth always lives in forest areas. He spends most of his life hanging down. The female sloth even feeds her **young** hanging from a tree branch. The sloth eats plants, leaves, and small green sticks from the tree he is hanging on.

1. **Underline the best title for this paragraph:**
   A Forest Animal
   A Green Plant
   The Slow, Slow Sloth

2. **Circle the answers you think are correct:**
   Some sloths spend more time sitting than hanging.　　　Yes　　No
   The plants that grow on the sloth make him look green.　　　Yes　　No

3. **Circle the correct meaning for each underlined word:**
   moss

   　　a. small green plants
   　　b. dead leaves
   　　c. sticks and branches

   young
   　　a. brothers and sisters
   　　b. mothers and fathers
   　　c. babies

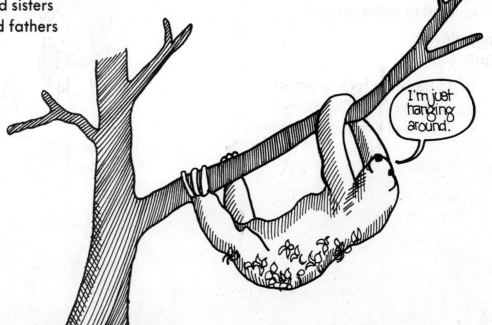

Did you know . . .
there are plants which eat small animals?

All plants can make their own food using air and sunshine as long as they have water and **minerals** from the soil. A few plants can also **lure** and trap small animals. After the animals have been turned into food which is used by the plant, the trap is **reset**. All of these plants can trap small animals such as an ant or a fly, but some plants can trap animals as big as young fish, mice, frogs, or even birds!

1. **Underline the best title for this paragraph:**
   Man-Eating Plants
   Animal-Eating Plants
   Plant-Eating Plants

2. **Fill in the blanks with the correct answers:**
   Name three animals some plants can trap:

   _____

   _____

   _____

   All plants need water and _____ from the soil.

3. **Circle the correct meaning for each underlined word:**
   minerals
   (min′er als)

       a. a natural chemical
       b. the sparkly part of soil
       c. the wet part of soil

   lure

       a. to trap
       b. to try to trap
       c. to work a trap

   reset
   (re′set)

       a. to remake
       b. to catch again
       c. to set again

Did you know . . .
that the seeds of an orchid are so small that many **hundreds** could fit on the head of a pin?

Many people think that the orchid is one of the most beautiful flowers in the world. There are more different kinds of orchids than any other plant in the world. Orchids grow in the warm, **tropic** places of the world. Most plants put roots into the ground to get food. But not the orchid. It often lives and grows on trees. It gets much of its food from the air. Orchids are both beautiful and **expensive.**

1. **Underline the best title for this paragraph:**
   The Orchid's Tiny Seeds
   Flowers of the World
   The Beautiful Orchid

2. **Circle the answers you think are correct:**
   The orchid grows on
      a. the ground
      b. the air
      c. trees

   There are only a few different kinds of orchids.   Yes   No

3. **Circle the correct meaning for each underlined word:**
   tropic
   (trop′ic)
      a. warm, wet places of the world
      b. warm, dry places of the world
      c. cool areas of the world

   hundreds
   (hun′dreds)
      a. a big flower
      b. a big number
      c. a big plant

   expensive
   (ex pen′sive)
      a. something to eat
      b. something that costs a lot
      c. something that does not cost a lot

Did you know . . .
people once used cows to buy things?

Before there was any money at all, people just traded with each other. One person who had honey might trade his honey for some cloth. A name for this kind of trade is **barter**. Later on, animals were money. People could pay their **taxes** with a cow. Salt was money. Corn, grain, shells, and tools were money, too. Finally, almost three thousand years ago, the first real money was made by the **government** of a country called Lydia. Now, only governments make money for people to use.

1. **Underline the best title for this paragraph:**
   Selling Cows
   Bartering
   Many Kinds of Money

2. **Circle the answers you think are correct:**
   Before there was money, people used a form of trade called:
   a. taxes
   b. cows
   c. barter
   The first real money was made three thousand years ago.   Yes   No

3. **Circle the correct meaning for each underlined word:**
   barter
   (bar′ter)

   a. to trade
   b. to pay with money
   c. to sell a cow

   taxes
   a. money owed to a storekeeper
   b. money owed to a farmer
   c. money owed to a government

   government
   (gov′ern ment)

   a. the way a country is ruled
   b. part of the country of Lydia
   c. the part of a country which makes money

 # Did you know . . .
that about 1,000 **tons** of meteorites land on the earth every day?

Meteorites are pieces of material from outerspace that fall to earth. The heat made when they fly through the earth's air makes some of them shine. If you saw one at night, you might call it a shooting star, though it is not a star at all. Most meteorites burn or break up before they ever land. What is left falls to earth in the form of small pieces of dust. Meteorites are the only real **clues** that today's scientists have to what outerspace is like and what it is made of.

1. **Underline the best title for this paragraph:**
   Shooting Stars
   Meteorites
   Dusty Places

2. **Circle the answer you think is correct:**
   Shooting stars are really:
   a. pieces of stars
   b. meteorites
   c. stones

3. **Circle the correct meaning for each underlined word:**
   ton
   a. one pound
   b. ten pounds
   c. 2,000 pounds

   clues
   a. hints
   b. pieces of meteorites
   c. dust

I'm not taking any chances!

Did you know . . .
that some Indians thought Mormon crickets were a tasty food?

The Mormon cricket is a large and **clumsy** bug that lives in the western United States. It is a very bad **pest** because it eats the grain crops, like wheat. Early settlers in Utah almost lost their **entire** crop of grain when the Mormon cricket came on them in huge numbers. But, just in time, flocks of sea gulls came. They ate the crickets and saved the grain. The Mormon cricket will eat anything it can find. That includes other Mormon crickets, if they get in the way.

1. **Underline the best title for this paragraph:**
    A Western Pest
    Gulls Eat Them
    A Tasty Food

2. **Circle the answers you think are correct:**
    Mormon crickets will eat Mormon crickets.　　　Yes　　No
    Mormon crickets live in the eastern part of the
    United States.　　　Yes　　No

3. **Circle the correct meaning for each underlined word:**
    clumsy
    (clum′sy)

    a. awkward
    b. big
    c. ugly

    pest
    a. something good to have around
    b. something bad to have around
    c. something you want for breakfast

    entire
    (en tire′)

    a. all, the whole
    b. part of
    c. none of

They're good but they keep jumping out of the pan!

 Did you know . . .
that the smallest deer in the world is only two feet
high at the shoulder?

The pudu deer of South America is that small. Now think of the largest deer in the world, the moose. He can be found in North America. His shoulders can be as tall as the ceilings in most houses. His head and huge antlers go even higher! Antlers are one thing that all deer have **in common**. They lose their old pair and grow a new pair each year. All through history deer have been an important **source** of food and fur for people.

1. **Underline the best title for this paragraph:**
   The Smallest Deer
   The Biggest Deer
   The Biggest and the Smallest Deer

2. **Fill in the blanks with the correct answers:**
   A deer's height is measured at his _____.
   Deer grow a new pair of _____ each year.

3. **Circle the correct meaning for each underlined word:**
   in common
       a. alike
       b. different
       c. ordinary

   source
       a. a type of deer for eating
       b. place to get something that is needed
       c. food and clothing

Now my grandma can stop calling me "little dear."

Did you know . . .
that the **marine** crocodile is so large, he could swallow a whole deer for his lunch?

The marine crocodile is found along the sea shores of the continent of Asia. And he is huge! He can grow to be almost as long as a school bus. He has large jaws, big teeth, strong legs, and a **powerful** tail. He uses that tail to move quickly along in the salt water where he lives. The marine crocodile spends most of his time eating. He will eat just about any animal he can catch.

1. **Underline the best title for this paragraph:**
   He's Big All Over
   He's a Big Eater
   He's Got Big Jaws

2. **Circle the answers you think are correct:**
   Marine crocodiles live mostly in America.　　　Yes　　　No
   The marine crocodile will eat anything.　　　Yes　　　No

3. **Circle the correct meaning for each underlined word:**
   marine
   (ma rine′)

   　a. having to do with crocodiles
   　b. having to do with water
   　c. having to do with large animals

   powerful
   (pow′er ful)

   　a. very large
   　b. very thick
   　c. very strong

I could go for a deerburger for lunch!

 Did you know . . .
that a bird called the Arctic tern migrates half way around the world each spring and fall, from near the North Pole almost to the South Pole?

Many types of birds **migrate**, or move from one place to another and back each year. Birds migrate to get away from the cold weather in the north and to find food. For some strange reason, many go much farther south than they need to. The length of days is one thing that tells birds it is time to move on. Before leaving, many birds grow an extra layer of fat to keep them going on the long trip. Birds find their way by following **landmarks**. They also use the stars and moon for direction.

1. **Underline the best title for this paragraph:**
   The Migrating Arctic Tern
   The Migrating Warbler
   Migrating Birds

2. **Fill in the blanks with the correct answers:**
   Most birds use the _____ and _____ to find their way when migrating.
   The _____ of days tells many birds when to migrate.

3. **Circle the correct meaning for each underlined word:**
   migrate
   (mi′grate)

   a. to move to a new place and stay there
   b. to move from one place to another and back
   c. to marry

   landmarks
   (land′marks)

   a. drawings on a map
   b. familiar places used to tell direction
   c. road signs

Let's see... turn left at the next star.

Did you know . . .
that the giant squid has the world's largest eye?

That is true! The eye of the giant squid is as big as a dinner plate. The giant squid has ten arms on his large head. Two of these arms have **suction** cups on the ends. The squid uses these suction cups to catch and hold the fish he eats. The giant squid also has his own way of scaring off his **predators.** When he is in danger, he squirts out a dark ink into the water. That mixes up the predator and gives the squid a chance to get away.

1. **Underline the best title for this paragraph:**
   The Inky Squid
   The Ten-Armed Squid
   The Giant Squid

2. **Fill in the blanks with the correct answers:**
   The giant squid has _____ arms with suctions cups.
   When in danger, the squid squirts out _____.

3. **Circle the correct meaning for each underlined word:**
   suction
   (suc′tion)

       a. blowing
       b. sucking
       c. spitting

   predators
   (pred′a tors)

       a. animals which kill the squid for food
       b. animals which kill the squid for fun
       c. animals which are friends of the squid

I'll bet he has a hard time finding sunglasses!

Did you know . . .
that an octopus likes best to be alone?

This scary looking sea animal is really very **gentle** and friendly. He likes to live alone in a crack or under a rock on the bottom of the sea. He catches his food, most often shellfish, with the suckers on his long arms. The female octopus is a very good mother. After laying her eggs, she is so busy taking care of them that she does not even eat. When the eggs hatch, she dies. Her work is done. In zoos the octopus has shown itself to be very **intelligent.**

1. **Underline the best title for this paragraph:**
   Octopus: The Loner
   Octopus: The Good Mother
   Under the Sea

2. **Circle the answers you think are correct:**
   The female octopus lays eggs.   Yes   No
   The octopus lives in large families.   Yes   No

3. **Circle the correct meaning for the underlined word:**
   gentle
   (gen´tle)

       a. soft, easy-going
       b. babyish
       c. many arms

   intelligent
   (in tel´li gent)

       a. good at swimming
       b. good looking
       c. smart

Did you know . . .
that the largest island in the world is Greenland?

The island of Greenland lies near the North Pole. It is almost all ice-covered. About the only place that is not covered with ice is the land along the **coast**. Even that land has very little **soil**, and so, very few trees or farms. Fishing and seal hunting are two of the most important jobs in Greenland. Only about 50,000 people live on the whole island. That is about as many as live in a small American city.

1. **Underline the best title for this paragraph:**
   A Green Island
   A Huge Island
   A Small American City

2. **Circle the answers you think are correct:**
   Most of Greenland is covered with:
   a. grass
   b. farms
   c. ice
   The island of Greenland has about 50,000 people.   Yes   No

3. **Circle the correct meaning for each underlined word:**
   coast
   a. the land along a park
   b. the land along the sea
   c. the land along a road

   soil
   a. some trees
   b. dirt for growing things in
   c. some people

Did you know . . .
that there are still many active volcanoes in the world today?

An active volcano is one that is still hot, and one that will still **erupt** every now and then. Volcanoes are holes in the cool upper layer of the earth through which hot, melted rock sometimes comes out. Some volcanoes just slowly **seep** melted rock called lava. Volcanoes which contain a lot of gas and steam will burst out lava like an explosion. The only active volcanoes in the United States are in Hawaii, Alaska, and in some mountains close to the Pacific Ocean.

1. **Underline the best title for this paragraph:**
    Hawaii's Volcanoes
    Hot Rock
    Active Volcanoes

2. **Circle the answers you think are correct:**
    There are active volcanoes all over the United States.   Yes   No
    Lava is melted rock.   Yes   No

3. **Circle the correct meaning for each underlined word:**
    erupt
    > a. to shoot off
    > b. to lay down
    > c. to die

    seep
    > a. to run in
    > b. to run out fast
    > c. to run out slowly

If we had a volcano in our yard... I wouldn't have to mow!

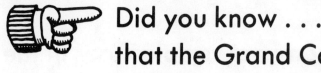

Did you know . . .
that the Grand Canyon is the most **popular** place to visit in the United States?

The Grand Canyon is a huge **canyon** in the state of Arizona. It was made a national park in 1919. If you stood on the edge at its deepest point, the bottom of the canyon would be one mile down. The Colorado River runs through the bottom of the Grand Canyon. It is this river, over many years, that cut the canyon deeper and deeper into the land. Wind and rain and ice also did their part in making the canyon what it is today.

1. **Underline the best title for this paragraph:**
   A Grand River
   A Huge Canyon
   A Busy River

2. **Fill in the blanks with the correct answers:**
   Name four things which made the Grand Canyon:
   _____
   _____
   _____
   _____

3. **Circle the correct meaning for each underlined word:**
   popular
   (pop′u lar)

   a. having to do with poplar trees
   b. having to do with canyons
   c. liked by most people

   canyon
   (can′yon)

   a. a huge gun used in wars
   b. a deep and narrow valley
   c. a wide river

It was the biggest hole we've ever seen!

 Did you know . . .
that Old Faithful geyser at Yellowstone Park
shoots up its spray of water more often than any
other geyser known?

Most geysers are not nearly so regular as Old Faithful. So you can see how this geyser got its name. Geysers are most often found where there were once **volcanoes** a few thousand years ago. You see the part of the geyser that is above the ground . . . the spray of hot water and steam. But a lot of the geyser you do not see . . . the part that is underground. Underground a geyser is a long, **narrow** hole that goes down deep, where the rock is very hot. That hot rock heats up the water of the geyser until it shoots off in a huge gush of water and steam.

1. **Underline the best title for this paragraph:**
   Near Old Volcanoes
   Geysers Above and Below
   A Narrow Hole

2. **Fill in the blanks with the correct answers:**
   Old Faithful got its name because it is so _____.
   The part of a geyser that you see is hot _____ and _____.

3. **Circle the correct meaning for each underlined word:**
   volcanoes
   (vol ca'noes)

   a. green mountains
   b. mountains that erupt melted rock
   c. tall mountains

   narrow
   (nar'row)

   a. not wide
   b. wide
   c. not short

Did you know . . .
that our oldest national park is Yellowstone?

In 1870 a group of people spent **several** weeks traveling through northwest Wyoming. One night they sat talking around a campfire. They could not believe some of the things they had seen in this beautiful country. Waterfalls, forests, deep canyons, tall geysers, wild animals . . . they saw them all. They felt that this place and its beauty should belong to all the people of America. They wanted it to be **preserved** just like it was for everyone to enjoy. Two years later Yellowstone was made our first national park.

1. **Underline the best title for this paragraph:**
   Beautiful Country
   For All to Enjoy
   Our First National Park

2. **Fill in the blanks with the correct answers:**
   The group of people were traveling in the state of _____.
   Yellowstone was made a national park in _____.

3. **Circle the correct meaning for each underlined word:**
   several
   (sev′er al)

   a. a few
   b. one
   c. seven

   preserved
   (pre served′)

   a. saved, kept in a natural way
   b. something sweet
   c. brought to the attention of

Did you know . . .
that the ceiling in the Big Room at Carlsbad Caverns is 22 **stories** high?

The Carlsbad Caverns, or caves, are in the state of New Mexico. There are many huge rooms with many hallways, all under the ground. Most of these caverns have not yet been explored. The building of these caverns began many millions of years ago. Water got into small, **hairline** cracks in the limestone. **Gradually**, the water made the cracks break, and the caverns were formed. Thousands of people are taken on trips to certain parts of the caverns every year.

1. **Underline the best title for this paragraph:**
   The Big Room
   Carlsbad Caverns' History
   Exploring Caverns

2. **Circle the answers you think are correct:**
   Most of the Carlsbad Caverns have been explored.   Yes   No
   Not very many people visit the caverns today.   Yes   No

3. **Circle the correct meaning for each underlined word:**
   stories

       a. caves
       b. floors in a building
       c. cracks

   hairline
   (hair′line)

       a. a very skinny, narrow line
       b. a very big line
       c. a part in a person's hair

   gradually
   (grad′u ally)

       a. quickly
       b. little by little
       c. somewhat

Thank goodness I don't have to dust up there!

Did you know . . .
that the only one to live through the battle at Little Big Horn was a horse?

More than 100 years ago, General Custer and 225 of his men died when they were attacked by Indians at Little Big Horn, Montana. The only **survivor** was the horse of one of the men. The name of the horse was Comanche. He had seven deep cuts. Some of the cuts were very serious, but he did not die. No one ever rode him again. He spent the rest of his life taking part in special **military** parades. He was 30 years old when he died. Comanche can now be seen at the University of Kansas.

1. **Underline the best title for this paragraph:**
    Little Big Horn
    Custer's Last Stand
    Comanche: The Only Survivor

2. **Circle the answers you think are correct:**
    More than 400 American soldiers died at Little Big Horn.   Yes   No
    You can see Comanche now at:
       a. Little Big Horn
       b. Indian Village
       c. University of Kansas

3. **Circle the correct meaning for each underlined word:**
    survivor
    (sur vi′vor)

       a. one who dies in battle
       b. one who makes it through a battle alive
       c. one who doesn't fight in battles

    military
    (mil′i tary)

       a. long
       b. army
       c. holiday

Did you know . . .
that the Statue of Liberty was a birthday present from France to the United States?

France gave us the Statue of **Liberty** as a present when the United States turned 100 years old in 1876. The copper statue was to be placed in the **harbor** of New York City. For years now it has been an exciting and sometimes tearful sight. People coming to our country for the first time see it. Soldiers returning from war know they are home when they see it. It welcomes everyone. The right hand of the statue holds a torch to light the way into the harbor. Its left hand holds a book which says July 4, 1776.

1. **Underline the best title for this paragraph:**
   Happy Birthday
   The Statue of Liberty
   A Tearful Sight

2. **Fill in the blanks with the correct answers:**
   The Statue of Liberty is made of _____.
   The Statue of Liberty was a present for our _____ birthday.

3. **Circle the correct meaning for each underlined word:**
   liberty
   (lib′er ty)

      a. joy
      b. fear
      c. freedom

   harbor
   (har′bor)

      a. a place for presents
      b. a place for statues
      c. a protected place where water comes into land

Did you know . . . that Mark Twain's real name was Samuel Clemens?

Mark Twain is **probably** the most popular American **author** ever. He wrote **Tom Sawyer** and **Huckleberry Finn.** Both books are about boys growing up in a riverboat town along the Mississippi River. Mark Twain grew up in that kind of town. A lot of what he wrote was about his own life as a young boy. As he got older, Mr. Twain worked at many different jobs. He was a printer, a riverboat pilot, a soldier, a **prospector** for gold, as well as a writer.

1. **Underline the best title for this paragraph:**
   The Writer Samuel Clemens
   Huckleberry Finn
   Tom Sawyer

2. **Circle the answers you think are correct:**
   Mark Twain lived on a lake as a boy.   Yes   No
   At one time Mark Twain worked as a mailman.   Yes   No

3. **Circle the correct meaning for each underlined word:**
   probably
   (prob′a bly)

   a. most likely
   b. not likely
   c. for sure

   author
   (au′thor)

   a. printer
   b. soldier
   c. writer

   prospector
   (pros′pec tor)

   a. one who sells gold
   b. one who looks for gold
   c. one who buys gold

Did you know . . . that "Dixie," the Southerner's song during the Civil War, was written by a Northerner?

Daniel Emmet was a **musician** born in a Northern state. He became a drummer boy in the army. He also played in many traveling bands. When he wrote "Dixie" in 1859, it was popular in both the North and the South. It made Mr. Emmet unhappy when the people of the South made it their song during the Civil War. The song **remained** a **favorite** of Southerners even after the war was over.

1. **Underline the best title for this paragraph:**
   A Great Musician
   "Oh, I Wish I Was in Dixie!"
   The Civil War

2. **Circle the answers you think are correct:**
   Daniel Emmett once played the drums in the army.　　Yes　　No
   People of the North enjoyed "Dixie" before the war.　　Yes　　No

3. **Circle the correct meaning for each underlined word:**
   musician
   (mu si′cian)

   a. one who writes music
   b. one who sings music
   c. one who is good at all types of music

   remained
   (re mained′)

   a. stayed
   b. left
   c. went away

   favorite
   (fa′vor ite)

   a. something liked more than the others
   b. something not liked very well
   c. something no one likes

Oh, I wish I was in Dixie!

Did you know . . .
that the spine-tailed swift, a bird of Asia, can fly over 100 miles an hour?

That is two times as fast as most cars travel on the expressway! The swift spends more time in the air than any other bird. He even catches and eats insects while flying. He has long, narrow wings and strong breast muscles. That makes it possible for him to fly for a long time without **tiring**. The swift will almost always land on something **vertical**, like a tree or a chimney. He will **seldom** land on the ground because it is too hard for him to take off from the ground.

1. **Underline the best title for this paragraph:**
   The Swift Swift
   The Insect-Eating Swift
   Eating in Flight

2. **Fill in the blanks with the correct answers:**
   The swift likes to eat _____.
   The swift usually lands on things like a _____ or _____.

3. **Circle the correct meaning for each underlined word:**
   tiring
   (tir′ing)

      a. putting tires on a car
      b. getting tired
      c. falling

   vertical
   (ver′ti cal)

      a. up and down
      b. across
      c. over and under

   seldom
   (sel′dom)

      a. sometimes
      b. all the time
      c. hardly ever

Page 1
1. Ahhhhhhh-Choooo
2. no
   no
3. particles a
   polite b

Page 2
1. Ice Skating Wasn't Just for Fun
2. no
   no
3. transportation a
   development c
   canals b

Page 3
1. Wearing Stilts
2. no
   no
3. soggy b
   chores a
   serious c

Page 4
1. The Beginning of Basketball
2. 1891
   janitor
3. instructor c
   invented a

Page 5
1. Growing Popcorn
2. Midwest
   movies
3. mainly b
   stalks c
   blizzard b

Page 6
1. All About Mushrooms
2. dead
   ring
3. varieties b
   edible c
   delicious a

Page 7
1. It Grows on Trees!
2. December
   maple, elm, apple
3. attaches b
   autumn a

Page 8
1. Peanuts for This and That
2. peanut butter
   Northern
3. dynamite a
   popularity b

Page 9
1. The Slow, Slow Sloth
2. no
   yes
3. moss a
   young c

Page 10
1. Animal-Eating Plants
2. ant, fly, fish, mice, frogs, birds
   minerals
3. minerals a
   lure b
   reset c

Page 11
1. The Beautiful Orchid
2. c
   no
3. tropic a
   hundreds b
   expensive b

Page 12
1. Many Kinds of Money
2. c
   yes
3. barter a
   taxes c
   government a

Page 13
1. Meteorites
2. b
3. ton c
   clues a

Page 14
1. A Western Pest
2. yes
   no
3. clumsy a
   pest b
   entire a

Page 15
1. The Biggest and the Smallest Deer
2. shoulder
   antlers
3. in common a
   source b

Page 16
1. He's Big All Over
2. no
   no
3. marine b
   powerful c

Page 17
1. Migrating Birds
2. stars, moon
   length
3. migrate b
   landmarks b

Page 18
1. The Giant Squid
2. two
   ink
3. suction b
   predators a

Page 19
1. Octopus: The Loner
2. yes
   no
3. gentle a
   intelligent c

Page 20
1. A Huge Island
2. ice
   yes
3. coast b
   soil b

Page 21
1. Active Volcanoes
2. no
   yes
3. erupt a
   seep c

Page 22
1. A Huge Canyon
2. river, wind, rain, ice
3. popular c
   canyon b

Page 23
1. Geysers Above and Below
2. faithful, regular
   water, steam
3. volcanoes b
   narrow a

Page 24
1. Our First National Park
2. Wyoming
   1872
3. several a
   preserved a

Page 25
1. Carlsbad Caverns' History
2. no
   no
3. stories b
   hairline a
   gradually b

Page 26
1. Comanche: The Only Survivor
2. no
   c
3. survivor b
   military b

Page 27
1. The Statue of Liberty
2. copper
   100th
3. liberty c
   harbor c

Page 28
1. The Writer Samuel Clemens
2. no
   no
3. probably a
   author c
   prospector b

Page 29
1. "Oh, I Wish I Was in Dixie!"
2. yes
   yes
3. musician c
   remained a
   favorite a

Page 30
1. The Swift Swift
2. insects
   tree, chimney
3. tiring b
   vertical a
   seldom c